THORN

Thorn

Heather Clauson and John Grebe

ELM HILL

A Division of
HarperCollins Christian Publishing

www.elmhillbooks.com

Thorn

Published in Nashville, Tennessee, by Elm Hill, an imprint of Thomas Nelson. Elm Hill and Thomas Nelson are registered trademarks of HarperCollins Christian Publishing, Inc.

Elm Hill titles may be purchased in bulk for educational, business, fund-raising, or sales promotional use. For information, please e-mail SpecialMarkets@ThomasNelson.com.

Library of Congress Cataloging-in-Publication Data

Library of Congress Control Number: 2018959313

ISBN 978-1-595559319 (Paperback)
ISBN 978-1-595559296 (Hardbound)
ISBN 978-1-595559418 (eBook)

To Hannah and Aidan

Thorn was a songbird who lived in Israel.

She spent her days gathering twigs, leaves, and grass for her nest.

Thorn also spent her days singing.

Thorn greeted every morning with songs of joy and closed every day with songs of praise.

On one particularly quiet morning, while Thorn was resting in an olive tree, a crowd was gathering in the street below.

A man was riding on a donkey through the crowd. The people were waving palm branches in the air and laying them down on the road.

The people were shouting, "Hosanna, blessed is He who comes in the name of the Lord!"

As the crowd celebrated the arrival of Jesus to Jerusalem, Thorn added her songs of joy to the celebration.

Thorn waited until the crowd was gone and then she picked up a palm branch and took it back to her nest.

Later in the week, Thorn spotted Jesus through a window. He was gathered with his friends in an upper room. They were sharing a meal together as Jesus passed around bread and a cup to his friends.

After the supper, Thorn followed Jesus and his friends to a garden. Jesus knelt down and began praying and weeping, but his friends lay sleeping around him. Thorn perched on a nearby rock and quietly sang songs of peace.

That night, a crowd came and took Jesus away.

The next day, Thorn arranged her nest to protect the eggs she had laid.

It started as a quiet Friday morning, but in the afternoon, everything changed.

Again, a crowd gathered on the street,
but this time, the crowd was angry.

The people were shouting, "Crucify him!
Crucify him!"

Jesus was carrying a heavy cross, slowly making his
way through the crowd.

He kept falling down, but the soldiers showed him
no mercy and forced Jesus to continue walking.

Thorn flew closer. Noticing the crown of thorns, she offered songs of comfort to Jesus. The soldiers batted her away.

As Jesus fell down, Thorn flew near him and used her chest feathers to wipe the blood away from Jesus's eyes.

As the crowd watched and cheered,
Jesus was led to a hill, nailed to the cross,
and left to die.

Thorn flew to the cross, perched herself near the face of Christ, and sang songs of peace and comfort until Jesus breathed his last breath.

When the crown of thorns fell off Jesus's head,
Thorn settled into the middle of it and fell asleep.

In the middle of the night, Thorn sensed danger. When she opened her eyes, she saw two bright eyes staring right at her.

The sand cat was fierce, and Thorn's heart started beating fast.

Thorn was too frightened to move and closed her eyes as the cat pounced towards her.

Thorn heard a distinct yelp, and fearing the worst, she opened her eyes.

To her surprise, the cat had landed on the thorns and was limping away. Thorn was so grateful that the crown of thorns had protected her.

She picked up the crown of thorns and took it home so it could protect her family, as well.

After Thorn wove the crown of thorns into her nest, she went to the river to wash Jesus's blood off her chest feathers.

Though Thorn washed and washed in the river, the red color would not come out of her feathers.

Thorn flew home and settled into her nest, waiting with her mate for their eggs to hatch.

The next day, when the eggs hadn't yet hatched, Thorn flew to the tomb where the body of Jesus had been placed.

When Thorn arrived at the tomb, she was surprised that the stone had been rolled away!

Thorn flew inside the tomb. It was empty! Jesus wasn't there and Thorn was overjoyed knowing that the Savior had been resurrected!

As she flew home to her nest, she looked down at her red feathers and realized the blessing of having the mark of Christ on her chest.

Later that day, the eggs hatched. Thorn sang songs of great jubilation as each of the baby birds was born with bright red chest feathers, carrying on the blessing of the mark of Christ.

Here are some suggested activities to support the themes throughout *Thorn*. We hope these inspire creativity and promote faith-centered artistic expression.

- Reference the Passion Week from Scripture and discuss it together.
- Read the story out loudly while children draw, color, and/or paint.
- Go on a walk to observe different types of nests in trees and on buildings.
- If you can sit and observe from a distance, watch birds interacting with one another.
- Build your own nest. Use clay, mud, sticks, leaves, and other child safe materials.
- Paint some pebbles or rocks to resemble eggs (add them to the nest you make).
- Do some research about the Israeli Bluethroat (Luscinia Svecica) and Desert Sand Cat.
- Listen to different bird calls and songs.

The two children, to whom this book is dedicated, overheard a conversation between the authors and illustrator. While listening to descriptions of the illustrations that would be included in this book, both of them began drawing their own pictures as they interpreted the story in their own imaginations. We have included their illustrations here to honor their faith-centered artistic expression, and to inspire others to interact with Scripture in creative ways.

Hannah, 6 years old

"Thorn is holding a palm branch, bringing it back to her nest."

"Thorn is in her nest with her three eggs."

"Thorn wiping blood from Jesus's head, and that is the hill with the crosses."

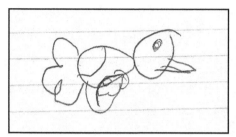

"Thorn is flying back to the nest with blood on her chest."

"That's the sand cat."

"Thorn facing the sand cat with her eyes shut and hearing a 'Yelp!'"

"That is the sand cat walking away, with the crown of thorns in Thorn's mouth."

"The palm branch is in her nest and she is about to land on her nest, bringing the crown of thorns back."

"Thorn flying away from her nest to go see Jesus."

*"Thorn is flying into
the tomb."*

Aidan, 4 years old

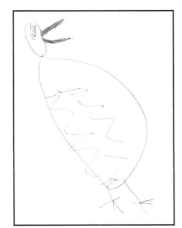

*"Thorn is happily
singing."*

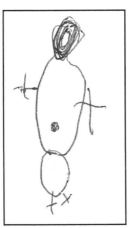

*"Jesus on the
cross."*

"Thorn's eggs."

CPSIA information can be obtained
at www.ICGtesting.com
Printed in the USA
LVHW061140211118
597897LV00003B/3/P